D0434914

Text copyright © 1989 Beverley Parkin
This illustrated edition copyright © 1989 Lion Publishing

Published by
Lion Publishing plc
Sandy Lane West, Littlemore, Oxford, England
ISBN 0 7459 1603 1
Lion Publishing Corporation
1705 Hubbard Avenue, Batavia, Illinois 60510, USA
ISBN 0 7459 1603 1
Albatross Books Pty Ltd
PO Box 320, Sutherland, NSW 2232, Australia
ISBN 0 7324 0123 2

First edition 1989

Bible Quotations from *The Holy Bible, New International
Version*: copyright ©.New York International Bible Society,
1978 and from the *Good News Bible*, copyright 1966, 1971 and
1976 American Bible Society, published by the Bible
Societies/Collins

Acknowledgments
Lion Publishing/David Alexander, cover and endpapers. All other photographs provided by NHPA:
J & M Bain (Buttercup); Jim Bain (Primrose); John Buckingham (Meadowsweet); G.J. Cambridge
(Clover, Knapweed, Toadflax, Self-heal); L. Campbell (Foxglove, Iris, Mallow, Poppy, Valerian);
Stephen Dalton (Dog Rose); Brian Hawkes (Convolvulus); E.A. Jones (Scarlet Pimpernel,
Nightshade); Michael Leach (Daisy, Dandelion); David Woodfall (Nettle, Rosebay Willow Herb)

British Library Cataloguing in Publication Data
Parkin, Beverley, *1936–*
    Flowers of the wayside.
    1. Christian life   2. Flowering plants
    I. Title
    248.4

    ISBN 0–7459–1603–1

Library of Congress Cataloging in Publication Data
Parkin, Beverley.
    Flowers of the wayside / Beverley Parkin. — 1st ed.
    p.   cm.
    ISBN 0–7459–1603–1
    1. Wild flowers—Religious aspects—Christianity—Meditations.
    I. Title.
    BV4832.2.P322   1989
    242—dc19

Printed in Singapore

July 23, 1992

Flowers of
the Wayside
BEVERLEY PARKIN

Dear Shirley

    I pray you will enjoy
relaxation, peace and hope
with the inspiration of this book.

Happy Birthday!

    The Lord Bless You,
      With Love, in Christ
          Dorothy Siemens

A LION BOOK
Oxford · Batavia · Sydney

Daisy

One day I wanted to be alone, to wander through our local woods and fields. As I quietly thanked God for the ability to walk and savour the scents and sounds, my eye was caught by a little clump of wild flowers almost hidden in the tall grass. As I bent over to appreciate their loveliness, a thought struck me. Here were flowers, beautiful, hidden, largely unappreciated – like so many people; ordinary people we would probably not look at twice – people quietly bringing up children or looking after elderly relatives. . . .

Daisies are among the most common of all our wild flowers. We crush them beneath our feet, decapitate them with our lawn mowers, and yet still they raise their heads. They are complex little flowers, opening with the light. They sprinkle grassy areas like a scattering of late snowflakes. But because they are so ordinary they are seldom appreciated.

Thinking of them I began to realize how much I had been helped and blessed by ordinary people. Maybe no book will ever be written about them, the media will show no interest in their lives. But these unknown people are precious individuals.

Maybe you are feeling hopeless and helpless, lonely or harassed, insignificant or unappreciated, crushed by people or circumstances. Let me tell you what God wants you to know: you are unique and precious in the sight of our Creator – Almighty God.

Heavenly Father, thank you that, although we are ordinary people and the world passes by, we are important to you.

66Are not two sparrows sold for a penny? Yet not one of them will fall to the ground apart from the will of your Father. And even the very hairs of your head are all numbered. So don't be afraid; you are worth more than many sparrows.99

FROM MATTHEW'S GOSPEL, CHAPTER 10

Yellow Iris

One of the plants I most look forward to seeing is the regal yellow iris. It grows in damp places, untroubled by storms and violent winds. There is great strength in its broad, spear-shaped leaves and the flowers bloom regardless of the weather. This was the flower that inspired the French kings' emblem, the 'Fleur de Lis'. The iris has great character. Unlike some of our more delicate wild plants, it won't allow us to ignore it.

I have met people like that, too. Like the iris, they stand straight and fearless, no matter what comes their way. Regardless of personal safety or reputation they are in the forefront of those who fight against injustice and stand up for the weak and afflicted.

The root of the iris has a cleansing effect. It was used as snuff, causing violent sneezing, to relieve sinus conditions. Taken internally it produced other violent reactions! It has never been a gentle medicine but it has always had its uses.

When Jesus walked upon the earth, he was seldom quiet. The Pharisees called him a revolutionary and a nuisance – even a heretic, who dared to heal people on God's day of rest. Today his followers still campaign for people in need. Society would be the poorer without these strong, compassionate characters – people who are unafraid of making themselves heard on behalf of those who cannot speak for themselves. Jesus spoke out constantly, teaching and demonstrating the love of God, and in the end he laid down his life for us all. That one violent act cleansed and keeps cleansing the lives of all those who trust in him.

Thank you Lord for those who are strong on behalf of others – we need them in our world.

"Speak up for those who cannot speak for themselves. . . defend the rights of the poor and needy.**"**

FROM PROVERBS, CHAPTER 31

Self-Heal

Self-heal, with its simple spiked flower, is one of the most useful of our wild herbs. Since it helped to staunch blood, it was used on battlegrounds, and to deal with wounds caused by hedgecutting or scything. A leaf bound on to the cut helped the healing process – hence the name Self-heal.

The idea of self-healing or self-help points to a special quality we all need – independence. Of course like most qualities it can be used or abused. A leaf from the plant will not stop someone bleeding to death! But the same leaf applied to a slight cut would be sensible: better than crying for help to all and sundry.

It's good to try to do or think things through for ourselves, to use our God-given intelligence to make up our own minds about issues, about people, about what we believe. Sometimes, however, we need help, to seek advice from a friend or someone with professional experience. Physical independence is valuable. Independence of mind is valuable. But to be independent of God brings spiritual poverty.

Father, thank you for the many ways in which we can help ourselves. But help us always to realize our dependence on you.

66Never let yourself think that you are wiser than you are; simply obey the Lord and refuse to do wrong. If you do, it will be like good medicine, healing your wounds and easing your pains.**99**

FROM PROVERBS, CHAPTER 3

White clover

I wonder if the little white clover knows what benefit it brings to mankind? As the dew evaporates from the tiny blossoms the bees move in hungrily, seeking all the nectar to store and take back to their hives. We harvest the resulting honey that is so good for us – but who remembers the insignificant flowers that have helped to produce such sweetness?

It is easy to ignore the white clover and concentrate on its more flamboyant purple sister. But what a shame that is! It is equally easy to ignore those people who keep in the background, quietly going about their daily tasks, sweetening life for their family, friends and neighbours, giving strength and energy to those who go out into the world of school, business and career. Honey itself, for all its uses, is often taken for granted – just as we take for granted the sweetness and strength of those who touch our lives in one form or another, often unrecognized.

I think of Ann, whose life brings these qualities to others. She dislikes being in the limelight and prefers to make her contribution unrecognized. But she was the first to encourage me to share God's love and she has helped many others develop their creative gifts. Ann is sweet without being sugary, strong without being overbearing, and full of concentrated energy! Perhaps you know someone like her?

For those who sweeten our lives and strengthen our spirits we thank you, Father. Help us to remember to say thank you to them.

❝Happy are those who are humble; they will receive what God has promised.**❞**

FROM MATTHEW'S GOSPEL, CHAPTER 5

Nettle

Stinging nettles are not the most popular of our wild plants. Yet they store tremendous quantities of energy-giving iron in their fearsome leaves. Gently simmered and eaten young, nettles are full of goodness. Of course, it's not so easy to be grateful for them when they've stung our hands, so a pair of stout gloves is advisable when picking them.

When I developed polio many years ago, neither I nor my parents could find anything good about it. But years later I can honestly say that it has added richness to my life. It has certainly taught me a lot about patience with myself, and hopefully with others.

Every second of every day someone comes face to face with a trauma that changes their lives. The diagnosis of diabetes, cancer or some other disease shocks, shatters and disables. How can we face up to these events? We cannot run away from them. Like the nettles, they have to be grasped and dealt with.

My own experience and the experience of others have helped many to realize that although at such a moment life appears to be at an end, God *is* in control. He never abandons us. In the midst of the trouble he is there, calming and strengthening, if we will only turn to him. I remember the story of Jesus standing up in the boat on the Sea of Galilee, calming the storm with the words 'Be still.' Such authority, such concern for his friends. His words provide the iron we need. If we allow God's power and love into any situation we can rest secure in the knowledge that our future is in his hands.

Almighty God, please calm the storm in our minds. Set us free from fear and bewilderment, and strengthen us in our sorrow and weakness. We put our future into your loving hands, this day and in the days that lie ahead.

❝May you be made strong with all the strength which comes from God's glorious power, so that you may be able to endure everything with patience.❞

FROM THE LETTER TO THE COLOSSIANS, CHAPTER 1

Mallow

This pretty pink flower was popular in Roman times as a cooked root vegetable eaten to prevent chest complaints. The soft leaves were bruised and bound onto body joints to promote the healing of inflamed tissues.

The mallow is often found at the road edge. The dust raised by passing traffic may dull its delicate petals, but the plant still lifts its courageous head, unmoved by noise and pollution.

Wondering what human quality could compare with this flower, I decided it must be a sense of humour! A good laugh relaxes the body and the mind. Of course, different kinds of humour appeal to different people. My family becomes quite hysterical watching slap-stick comedy, while I sit there with a dead-pan expression! But clever verbal wit can make me helpless with laughter! Cheap sick humour demeans those who are involved, but laughing at ourselves can help us keep a sense of proportion.

My mother has a great gift when it comes to relating incidents that have happened to her. Sometimes the situation has been quite traumatic but her sense of humour enables her to bring out the funny side in the retelling. Given the gift of humour, even painful emotions can be soothed and a new perspective brought to the situation.

What a joy it is to see smiling faces, to enjoy a joke. With so many desperately sad times in life, we need the lighter moments. Humour can touch us all. Laughter draws us together and it can help to heal so many difficult situations. It is as common and everyday as the mallow – and just as invaluable.

Thank you, God, for the gift of laughter. Help us to use it to lighten burdens and to cheer the sad, to strengthen and heal – and to take ourselves less seriously.

66Being cheerful keeps you healthy. It is slow death to be gloomy all the time.**99**

FROM PROVERBS, CHAPTER 17

Wild Rose

I have recently become re-acquainted with my thirteen-year-old niece, Kerina. She has an enthusiasm and energy for shopping and sight-seeing which I find quite exhausting! The rose oil she bought to fill a vapouriser was generously applied to the house, the furniture and even the dogs! And she returned to Canada on a waft of rose perfume! But while she was with us her joy in living was infectious, and her spirit of enquiry led us into places and events which enriched us all.

The quick-growing wild rose clambers enthusiastically through hedges and around copses, bearing clusters of charmingly simple pink blossoms which eventually give way to rich, red berries full of Vitamin C – good for birds and for growing children.

As we grow older, how important it is for us to retain some of the simple enthusiasm and joy in living we had as children. To remember grass taller than oneself, making daisy chains, the joy of rock pools, the breath-taking glimpse of a storm in full rage – with a trusted adult to protect us and provide the warmth and security of a goodnight kiss. As the years go by we take so much for granted. We need to recapture that freshness and newness which does not have to disappear with youth.

Lord God, help us to become as little children in your sight, enthusiastic to do your bidding, trusting you in all things and taking joy in your love and provision for us all.

❝Remember this! Whoever does not receive the Kingdom of God like a child will never enter it.**❞**

FROM LUKE'S GOSPEL, CHAPTER 18

Primrose and Cowslip

When we find demure clumps of primrose flowering on banks, or sheltering shyly in the grass ready to burst forth, we know that warmer weather is on the way. What joy! The world of nature creaks and groans into another year and we breathe a sigh of relief that winter is passing.

After the primrose, its cousin the cowslip will edge its way into the light – its golden umbrel swaying gently in the breeze, its perfume fragrant and exciting. Cowslip wine has always been popular amongst countryfolk, to enjoy for its own sake, and also to relieve headaches and insomnia. It provides a sedative to counterbalance nature's busiest season.

When life is at its busiest there is often most need to quieten down, to find peace when there seems no end to the frenetic activity going on all around. I like to discipline myself just to wander for an hour, especially in the spring, to find primroses and a cowslip or two and to breathe in their fragrance.

I find quietness in nature, and I appreciate it in people too. Jacqueline possesses this special quality for me. Her loving, tranquil face, her practical qualities derived from long experience of nursing and teaching, the compassion which drew her to work among refugee children, and her experience of bereavement have given her a tranquillity and repose which calms and quietens many troubled lives.

Jesus says that we may come to him for peace. It is his gift to us – not peace as the world understands it, but that peace of mind which comes from trusting in him.

Thank you God for the oasis of peace that you provide in the midst of chaos and noise. Thank you for your peace, which can be ours, whatever the circumstances.

66Peace I leave with you; my peace I give you. I do not give to you as the world gives. Do not let your hearts be troubled and do not be afraid.**99**

FROM JOHN'S GOSPEL, CHAPTER 14

Knapweed

The knapweed has many country names: 'hardhead', 'loggerhead' or 'iron head' are just some of them. The purple fringed flowers stand out by the wayside, and as the flower dies it is replaced by dry, silvery bracts, useful in dried flower arranging. Once it was used in an ointment for wounds and in medicine for catarrh. It was also eaten with pepper, to stimulate the appetite. The name 'hardhead' is derived from the firm, compact, tile-like flower base.

I discovered, many years ago, that I had a lot in common with the knapweed. I too was hard-headed, obstinate and stubborn. I like to go my own way. Maybe you have this problem too? It's a serious one, because what God asks is that we go *his* way. Self-centredness and hardness of heart spoils that relationship with God for which each of us was made.

Robert was one who chose his own way. He deliberately turned away from God. Having made an unsuitable marriage he set himself single-mindedly to make money. The result was restlessness and depression. For we are not made to live in total self-dependence but in relationship with God. In the end Robert realized that, and came back into God's family.

There will be times when each of us goes our own way, like Robert. But we can take heart. God never willingly lets us go. He warns us, and warms and softens our hearts and minds until we become responsive to him once again.

Heavenly Father, when we are hard, soften us; when we turn away, draw us back to yourself. Thank you for your patience and love.

66While the son was still a long way off, his father saw him an was filled with compassion for him. . . he said to his servants: 'Let's have a feast and celebrate. For this son of mine was dead and is alive again; he was lost and is found.'**99**

THE PARABLE OF THE LOST SON, FROM LUKE'S GOSPEL, CHAPTER 15

Toadflax

The world is a noisy place. Quite apart from planes, radios, TV, stereos, electrical gadgets and such like, everyone – including me – seems to have such a lot to say! Mouths open and close all day, emitting sounds which may or may not be helpful to another's ears or understanding. TV soap operas are full of verbal conflict. Every episode leaves us breathless to know how the situation will be resolved. Shouting and verbal abuse become part of our day.

Thankfully, plants don't shout – but some of them do have mouths! Toadflax has a tall stem, bearing yellow flowers. It is often called snap-dragon or wild antirrhinum. Each flower can be manipulated like a mouth, to open and close. Toadflax was once used to heal digestive upsets, calming inner turmoil.

Our own mouths can pour out poison, or bring calm. How do we use our tongues? It is so easy to gossip, to slander, to discourage, to pull down and tear apart another person's reputation or self-image. But we can also encourage and build up. We can give praise and express appreciation.

It is a real gift from God to have a friend like that – one who encourages. Eileen is a person like that. Over the years I, and many others, have been helped and encouraged by her, and she has defused many an explosive situation. Her words are a blessing. Are yours? Are mine? Jesus said that the tongue is a real giveaway: it's what comes out of our mouths that tells the world what we are really like.

Heavenly Father, grant us sensitivity and wisdom in our conversations. May we never think ourselves better than we are.

66The tongue has the power of life and death.**99**

FROM PROVERBS, CHAPTER 18

Foxglove

In winter, when I sit gazing into a roaring fire, with sparkling frost turning the ground into hard white diamonds beyond the door, it is an effort to remember the foxgloves that grow in abundance around this house. Tall and sturdy, with pink and white speckled flowers, the foxglove is one of my favourite flowers. It also produces the drug digitalis, long used to alleviate heart complaints.

But there are troubles of the heart no drug can help. The deepest heartache of all is bereavement. Loving makes us vulnerable, and when we lose someone we love, the searing, hurting pain leaves us bewildered and shocked. The only medicine that helps, as we fight our way through the depths of despair, is the knowledge that God loves and cares for us, that he will enable us to cope, minute by minute, day by day.

A friend of mine was devastated by the death of his wife. He is still often overwhelmed by grief. In the early days he felt that God had moved far away. Now he realizes that God was there all the time – he never changes. It was George who had changed. He felt that God had not kept his word. Over the years, instead of rejecting God, he has allowed the words of Scripture and his experience of living to ease the pain.

The life-saving drug digitalis comes from an ordinary common flower. It brings a better quality of life to many. But God's love is better than any drug. No condition is beyond his aid. He understands our tears and the cries of the heartbroken. And he has promised never to leave or forsake us.

Father, sometimes we hurt and the pain is suffocating. Please help us to get through this day, this night. Hold us tight and assure us of your continuing, caring presence with us.

"Even though I walk through the valley of the shadow of death, I will fear no evil, for you are with me.**"**

FROM PSALM 23

Nightshade

Before winter sets in, the hedgerows are full of coloured berries. Strings of red and orange woody nightshade beckon birds. The shiny black berries of the deadly nightshade tempt the unwary to taste its fruit. The poisonous berries can be fatal for children and most uncomfortable for adults, yet this plant yields an extract called belladonna that has the effect of enlarging the pupils so that the eye can be examined.

Many years ago I had an accident which caused me to lose my sight for a week or two. I was only too aware of the restrictions it placed upon my life. Having had only this small experience, I was humbled to meet an elderly blind lady who told me she had prayed daily for our family since our first and only meeting a few years previously. As I looked at her gentle, lined face and her unseeing, bright blue eyes, I was struck not by her blindness but by her spiritual vision and insight.

As her hands caressed the flowers I placed in her lap, my own eyes were opened a little more. I began to understand that, although physical blindness is a dreadful disability, stunted spiritual and emotional vision can be a great deal worse. Drops of belladonna enlarge the pupils of our eyes, but it is the work of God to open our eyes in the deeper sense, to see his truth and to enlarge our understanding of the spiritual dimension to life. He does so – often as we read the Bible, his word to us, and as we open ourselves to him in prayer.

Lord God, please give us spiritual vision, eyes to see and understand your purposes. May your love, your words and your power guide us in our lives.

❝I will lead the blind by ways they have not known, along unfamiliar paths I will guide them; I will turn the darkness into light before them and make the rough places smooth. These are the things I will do; I will not forsake them.**❞**

FROM ISAIAH 42

Buttercup

For many of us a field of buttercups glistening in the sunlight is the very essence of summer. As a child I used to hold a buttercup under a friend's chin and, if it reflected yellow (which it always did!), I would cry triumphantly, 'You like butter.'

But all is not what it seems. Buttercups are in fact poisonous. The juice in the root raises blisters on sensitive skins, and the leaves, which used to be placed on joints inflamed by rheumatism, can cause nasty skin ulcers. The beauty of the buttercup is no more than skin-deep!

In humans, too, a beautiful face may merely mask the bitterness of grief fermenting within. I think of the cry of a woman, sexually abused herself as a child, on discovering that her own two daughters were being abused by their father. I think of the much-loved childless aunt whose heart is torn with grief at the sight of babies she cannot produce herself. I think of the old and lonely who yearn to see or hear from their children and to know they are remembered. I think of the wife who knows that her mentally unstable husband will beat her at night, but who cannot bring herself to leave him.

So many conditions of the human heart are hidden beneath a placid surface. We should not let appearances deceive us. But even when no one else knows, God sees right through to the hurting emotions. He sees and he offers each of us his own strength and help and comfort. He has the power, if we will let him, to bring not only calm but healing, relieving the hurts and tensions that can so easily poison.

Dear God, deal with our innermost pain and help us to become in reality the people we long to be.

66Man looks at the outward appearance, but the Lord looks at the heart.**99**

FROM 1 SAMUEL, CHAPTER 16

Scarlet pimpernel

This tiny little flower, nestling in the grass, is an old-time weather forecaster. When the sun is out it opens its scarlet petals and soaks in the warmth and light. At the first hint of inclement weather, the flower furls itself tightly round the five vulnerable stamens, becoming indistinguishable from its leaves.

Many of us are equally prone to withdraw into ourselves when we face situations we do not like. We simply shut the door on the reality of the world. Mary subconsciously retreated into anorexia to avoid growing up. Joan became addicted to tranquillizers after her mother's death.

Extract of scarlet pimpernel was once given to those suffering from depression. Depression is a terrible thing – the sense of living within a great black cloud; the tears that flow for no reason. It is hard to get up in the morning and face the day ahead. How like the scarlet pimpernel that curls up into darkness when weather threatens it.

Many people also withdraw from God. They feel bitter and angry that he seems to show no interest or compassion towards them and their circumstances. And so they cut themselves off from the one who can help them most.

Few of us go through life without some circumstances which sadden us and tempt us to withdraw. I personally often find it hard to cope. But, like that little flower responding to the sun, we need to lift our heads and seek God's help, which is always close at hand.

Thank you, Father, that you want to coax us out of darkness and bring us into the light of life.

66There is nothing in all creation that will ever be able to separate us from the love of God which is ours through Christ Jesus our Lord.**99**

FROM THE LETTER TO THE ROMANS, CHAPTER 8

Convolvulus

onvolvulus has a pretty flower. This plant grows
healthily by winding itself onto a stronger stem, which
carries it up into the sunshine, where it can flourish.
One variety has large white trumpets; another has small pink-
flushed blossoms that straggle through meadows, twining their
stems round any convenient host plant. Convolvulus or
bindweed is one of the gardener's worst enemies. For the root
goes deep, and any piece of it left in the ground will grow
again. Seeds that set and fall into the soil remain viable for
twenty years.

Bitterness is like the bindweed. Many experiences in life
can make us bitter if we let them, because bitterness coils itself
around our emotions and reactions and is very difficult to
remove. It can really strangle our lives. But it grows strong only
if we let it.

I have met many people who have been through the trauma
of divorce and whose wounds have remained open for years.
Women have told me of the bitterness and resentment that has
robbed them of all joy. A sense of rejection causes some to turn
away from any loving gesture.

How can we avoid bitterness? We all make mistakes. We
give pain. We share in shattered illusions. We need to be
purged of bitterness and the self-pity that damages our emotions
and our health. We may feel helpless. Despite all our own
efforts, the bitterness remains. Yet if we are willing to ask God's
help, he will work a miracle in our hearts and minds, digging
out the root of bitterness and setting us free.

*Lord, we give you our bitterness and rejection. Forgive us
and make us able to forgive others. Heal our hurts and
help us to begin again.*

“Forgive us the wrongs we have done, as we forgive the
wrongs that others have done to us.**”**

FROM THE LORD'S PRAYER: MATTHEW'S GOSPEL, CHAPTER 6

Valerian

A walk along a river bank in summer reveals the towering stems of the valerian plant. The flowers are pink or flesh coloured and their dark green leaves provide a rich background for other marshy plants. Flowers and foliage spring from a rhizome deep in the ground and it is this that produces an antispasmodic drug used by herbalists to assist in muscle cramps and in cerebro-spinal disturbances.

I have met people with cerebral palsy who suffer a lot of distress from cramp. Spasmodic movements also cause pain, and not being able to use their limbs freely leads to acute frustration. The minor frustrations we all experience are nothing to the frustration those who are physically handicapped have to suffer. To take one tiny example, can you imagine having a terrible itch and not being able to scratch, or perhaps even to communicate your need to another person?

Valerian can sooth and quieten a jerky nervous system, but it cannot deal with a frustrated spirit – only God can do that.

I think of John, who despite enormous difficulties produces writing of great insight and wisdom; of Mary, whose foot paintings give so much pleasure; of Pat and Ian, whose marriage is based on love and understanding of each other's physical weaknesses. Each of these people can speak of God's power to soothe the spirit in the midst of bodily frustration. Their lives enrich us all.

Dear Father, so often we feel utterly frustrated at not being able to control our own bodies or desires. Soothe us with your understanding and help us to count our blessings.

❝Why am I so sad? Why am I so troubled? I will put my hope in God, and once again I will praise him, my saviour and my God.**❞**

FROM PSALM 42

Rosebay willow herb

At first sight fire-scorched earth appears to be totally arid. But, as the season moves on, a miracle takes place. First, tiny green leaves burst through the blackened earth, and soon the whole area is ablaze with tall plants bearing pinnacles of pink blooms. Rosebay willow herb or 'fireweed' transforms woodland clearances, bomb-sites and wasteland into a feast for the eyes.

Fireweed has always been a bonus for country folk. The root contains tannin for preserving. Ale may be made from the soft, sweet pith of the stems. And delicate skins, washed in an infusion of roots and leaves, retain their softness and pliability. At one time the fluffy white seedheads were mixed with cotton fibre to make stockings and pillow stuffings. A very practical, housewifely plant!

But the rosebay willow herb has an easier lesson to teach. It's a survivor that thrives on reclaiming barren places. It reminds us that out of material crises a new lifestyle may emerge. They do not have to make us embittered or sour. We can make the crisis a thing of beauty and creativity. It can produce practical qualities of compassion, humour, self-control, patience and faith in God.

In the past, our home has been damaged by fire, my husband has been out of work, and various crises have arisen. But with God's help these things have given us a new sense of the true priorities. This can be your experience too, as you face your particular patch of fire-scorched ground.

When our world is shaken by circumstance, please help us, Father, to face the future and turn the bleakness into beauty, shock into strength.

66The fruit of God's Spirit is love, joy, peace, patience, kindness, goodness, faithfulness, gentleness and self-control.**99**

FROM THE LETTER TO THE GALATIANS, CHAPTER 5

Meadowsweet

S ister Hilda is a Benedictine nun, living in a convent in North Wales. I received an unexpected letter from her and later we had the opportunity of meeting. Supported by a walking frame, she came towards me with a big smile and twinkling brown eyes. She is so tiny and fragile it seemed as if a puff of wind would cause her to fly away! Many illnesses have racked her small body and yet her spirit is strong and sweet.

Hilda has lived for the major part of her adult life in this quiet, enclosed order of nuns. She is such a chatterbox, it must have been a great discipline for her! The life of these nuns is filled with the sacrificial love and purity of Jesus. And they enrich the lives of all who meet them. The letters I receive from Sister Hilda reveal a quality of courage, patience, humility and joy in adversity which fills me with admiration.

When I see the fragrant meadowsweet, blooming at the roadside or in ditches, the pure snowy-capped plants remind me of this elderly nun who spends her life – unseen – pouring forth praises to God and praying for those who suffer in the world, or know only darkness and fear. In times long ago, meadowsweet was strewn over the floors of country houses, to bring perfume and cleansing to the stuffy, dark interiors. That too reminds me of Sister Hilda. We are not all called to her life, but I am so grateful for the prayers pouring forth from that abbey in Wales.

Father, help us to open our hearts in thanksgiving and praise. Whatever our circumstances may we bring joy and fragrance to the lives of others and show forth your purity in the world we live in.

❝Since you are God's dear children – you must try to be like him. Your life must be controlled by love, just as Christ loved us and gave his life for us as a sweet-smelling offering and sacrifice that pleases God.❞

FROM THE LETTER TO THE EPHESIANS, CHAPTER 5

Dandelion

Τ he dandelion is a very busy little plant. The flower makes wine, the leaves are rich in iron, the root is used for making dandelion coffee, and as an infusion has remarkable cleansing properties. The dandelion makes sure of its survival, too. As the flower matures, the wind takes its fluffy parachute seeds and sends them spinning through the air to a new home – starting the cycle once again.

For many of us, being busy and useful is tremendously important. In the family and in society, there is always something waiting to be done – meals to prepare, people to visit, housework, letters to be written – often a career too. Social needs cry out for action. Compassion drives us to participate in one area after another, in an endeavour to make the world a better place.

The sense of being useless which illness or circumstance may bring usually results in feelings of desolation and lack of confidence. But even the busy dandelion rests during the winter months, drawing nourishment from the surrounding soil, ready for the next great burst of energy.

God has created us to help one another. The Bible is full of instructions on how to live useful and purposeful lives. But we must not become so bound up in activity that we forget God and our relationship with him. Like the dandelion we need time to rest, time to set aside – if only a few minutes a day – to draw strength and guidance for the tasks that lie ahead, and to enjoy God's love.

Dear Father, we thank you for the privilege of work. But help us not to make it the be-all and end-all of life. Help us always to have time for you.

❝Remind me each morning of your constant love, for I put my trust in you. My prayers go up to you; show me the way I should go.❞

FROM PSALM 143

Red poppy

The seeds of the red poppy may lie dormant for many years. But as soon as the ground is disturbed they spring into life. Many a new motorway offers scarlet-mantled banks and verges, lavish only during its first year. Fields of poppies are a glorious sight. In Europe poppies are cultivated for their seeds, which are used in cakes, sprinkled on bread, or processed into oil. They also bloom where battles have been fought, and Remembrance Day with its symbolic poppy brings pain and pride to those who have lost loved-ones in war.

It is good to respect and remember those who have died for their country. Hopefully, by remembering the human cost, we will in future negotiate with words rather than weapons.

But there is one who gave his life for us all, that we might live and enjoy abundant life. When Jesus died on the cross, he took the whole weight of human sin and suffering upon himself. He overcame death once and for all. He gave us freedom, so that we need not live in fear. The good news of the Christian message is the seed from which new life grows for anyone willing to accept God's gift.

The love of God does not change, and through the centuries millions of ordinary people have experienced this new quality of life that changes and redirects them. The same power that raised Jesus from death to life is available to us in daily living.

Almighty God, thank you for Jesus who laid down his life that we might live. Take us, just as we are, and sow your new life within us, that we may know your forgiveness.

66As Scripture says, 'All mankind are like grass, and all their glory is like wild flowers. The grass withers, and the flowers fall, but the word of the Lord remains for ever.' This word is the Good News that was proclaimed to you.**99**

FROM THE FIRST LETTER OF PETER, CHAPTER 1